THE COMPLETE WATERBATH

CANNING COOKBOOK

TABLE OF CONTENTS

INTRODUCTION TO WATERBATH CANNING

Waterbath canning is a traditional food preservation method that uses a boiling water canner to process high-acid or acidic foods in sealed jars. This process effectively prevents the growth of spoilage microorganisms and extends the shelf life of foods. The primary purpose of waterbath canning is to create a vacuum-sealed environment within the jars, inhibiting the growth of bacteria, yeasts, and molds, and preserving the flavor, texture, and nutritional value of the food.

Types of Foods Suitable for Waterbath Canning:

a. Waterbath canning is ideal for preserving high-acid or acidic foods, which include fruits, fruit juices, jams, jellies, and pickled vegetables.

b. Examples of foods suitable for waterbath canning include berries, citrus fruits, tomatoes (with added acidity), and various types of relishes and chutneys.

ESSENTIAL EQUIPMENT

Canning Jars and Lids:

Canning jars, typically made of glass, are essential for waterbath canning. They come in various sizes and shapes, allowing flexibility in preserving different types of foods. Two-piece canning lids, consisting of a flat metal lid and a screw band, create an airtight seal when properly processed. Understanding the proper use and preparation of these lids is crucial for successful canning.

Waterbath Canner:

The waterbath canner is a large, deep pot specifically designed for waterbath canning. It comes with a fitted lid and a rack to keep the jars elevated and ensure even heat distribution during processing. The canner is filled with water, and jars are submerged in boiling water for a specified period, allowing the heat to penetrate the contents of the jars and eliminate any potential pathogens.

Other Necessary Tools and Utensils:

a. Funnel: A wide-mouthed funnel facilitates the easy and clean transfer of foods into canning jars.

b. Jar lifter: This specialized tool helps to lift and maneuver hot jars safely in and out of the waterbath canner.

c. Headspace tool: Ensures that the correct amount of headspace is maintained in each jar, preventing issues like improper sealing.

Waterbath canning is a preservation technique that involves processing high-acid or acidic foods in sealed jars submerged in a boiling water bath. The primary goal is to create a vacuum seal within the jars, effectively preventing the growth of spoilage microorganisms and ensuring the long-term stability of the preserved foods. Waterbath canning is a time-honored method that combines science, tradition, and practicality. It enables individuals to capture the essence of seasonal produce, preserve it safely, and savor the flavors of homegrown or locally sourced foods throughout the year. This method is commonly employed for fruits, fruit juices, jams, jellies, and pickled vegetables.

Purpose: The purpose of waterbath canning is multifaceted, aiming to achieve several key objectives:

Microbial Preservation: Waterbath canning is specifically designed for foods with high acidity, creating an environment hostile to the growth of bacteria, yeasts, and molds. The combination of high acidity and the heat generated during processing helps eliminate potential spoilage microorganisms.

Extended Shelf Life: By sealing foods in airtight jars, waterbath canning significantly extends the shelf life of the preserved items. This allows individuals to enjoy seasonal fruits and vegetables throughout the year, reducing waste and promoting sustainability.

Retention of Flavor and Nutritional Value: The canning process aims to retain the natural flavors, textures, and nutritional content of the foods being preserved. Heat from the boiling water penetrates the contents of the jars, facilitating preservation while maintaining the quality of the food.

Economical and Sustainable: Waterbath canning is a cost-effective and environmentally friendly way to manage surplus produce. It enables individuals to take advantage of seasonal abundance, reducing reliance on commercially processed foods and promoting self-sufficiency.

Customization and Creativity: Home canners have the flexibility to customize recipes, experiment with flavors, and create unique preserves, jams, and pickles. Waterbath canning empowers individuals to tailor recipes to personal preferences and dietary restrictions.

Gifts and Sharing: Canned goods make thoughtful and personalized gifts. Waterbath canning allows individuals to share the fruits of their labor with friends and family, creating a sense of community and connection through homemade, handcrafted foods.

Emergency Preparedness: Waterbath canning contributes to emergency preparedness by providing a stash of shelf-stable, nutritious foods that can be readily available in times of need. This aspect is particularly important for those who wish to build a resilient pantry.

TYPES OF FOODS SUITABLE FOR WATERBATH CANNING

Waterbath canning is a preservation method well-suited for high-acid or acidic foods. It's important to note that low-acid foods, such as most vegetables and meats, require a different canning method, such as pressure canning, due to the risk of botulism. Waterbath canning is best reserved for high-acid foods to ensure the safety and quality of the preserved items. The high acidity in these foods creates an environment that inhibits the growth of harmful microorganisms, making them safe for waterbath canning. Here are some types of foods that are particularly suitable for waterbath canning:

Fruits:

Berries: Strawberries, blueberries, raspberries, and blackberries are popular choices for jams, jellies, and preserves.

Stone Fruits: Peaches, plums, cherries, apricots, and nectarines can be canned as slices, halves, or in the form of fruit preserves.

Apples: Apples can be canned as applesauce, apple butter, or sliced for pie fillings.

Citrus Fruits: Oranges, lemons, limes, and grapefruits can be used to make citrus marmalades and fruit preserves.

Fruit Juices:

Berry Juices: Juices from berries, such as grape juice or raspberry juice, can be preserved using waterbath canning techniques.

Apple Juice: Homemade apple juice can be canned for later use in beverages or cooking.

Citrus Juices: Lemonade and other citrus-based juices can be preserved in jars.

Jams and Jellies:

Mixed Fruit Jams: Combining different fruits, like berries or stone fruits, can result in delicious mixed fruit jams.

Fruit Jellies: Using fruit juices, such as apple or grape juice, to create clear jellies with a variety of flavors.

Pickled Vegetables:

Cucumbers: Pickles are a classic waterbath canning item, with variations like dill pickles, bread and butter pickles, and sweet pickles.

Carrots: Carrot sticks or slices can be pickled with various spices for a crunchy snack.

Cauliflower and Peppers: These can be combined in colorful pickled mixes.

Salsas and Relishes:

Tomato Salsas: Salsas made with tomatoes, peppers, onions, and herbs can be preserved for use in cooking or as a condiment.

Fruit Salsas: Mango or peach salsas with a touch of heat can be waterbath canned for a unique twist.

Zesty Relishes: Onion, pepper, and cucumber relishes add a burst of flavor to dishes and can be preserved using waterbath canning.

Chutneys:

Spiced Fruit Chutneys: Chutneys made from a combination of fruits, spices, and vinegar create versatile condiments for meats and cheeses.

ESSENTIAL EQUIPMENT

Canning Jars: Glass jars are used to hold and preserve the food. They come in various sizes and shapes. Choose jars appropriate for the type of food being canned. Ensure jars are free from cracks or chips to guarantee a proper seal.

Canning Lids and Bands: Two-piece canning lids consist of a flat metal lid and a screw band. Lids create an airtight seal when processed correctly. Always use new lids for each canning session, and ensure they are free from dents or defects. Bands can be reused as long as they are in good condition.

Waterbath Canner: A large, deep pot designed for waterbath canning. It typically comes with a fitted lid and a rack to hold and elevate the jars during processing. Choose a canner large enough to comfortably accommodate the number of jars you plan to process. The rack is essential for ensuring even heat distribution around the jars.

Canning Funnel: A wide-mouthed funnel is used to transfer foods into jars without spillage, keeping the jar rims clean. Stainless steel or plastic funnels are common choices. Make sure the funnel is wide enough for the ingredients you are canning.

Jar Lifter: A specialized tool with gripping tongs used to lift and lower hot jars in and out of the waterbath canner. Ensure the jar lifter is designed for secure grip and heat resistance to prevent accidents during handling.

Headspace Tool: A tool for measuring and maintaining the correct amount of headspace in each jar. Headspace is the space between the food and the top of the jar. Headspace tools come in various forms, including measuring guides or rulers. Maintaining proper headspace is crucial for achieving a good seal.

Bubble Remover and Debubbler: A tool for releasing trapped air bubbles from the jar, ensuring even filling and preventing potential issues with sealing. A plastic or wooden tool with a flat end is often used for this purpose.

Timer: To keep track of processing times during canning. Use a reliable timer or a kitchen timer to ensure accurate processing times.

Kitchen Towels or Cloths: Towels are used for various purposes, such as wiping jar rims, handling hot jars, or protecting surfaces. Have a few clean, lint-free towels available for different tasks during the canning process.

Ladle: Used for scooping and pouring hot liquids, such as syrups, brines, or sauces, into jars. Choose a heat-resistant ladle with a pouring spout for precision.

Non-metallic Spatula or Bubble Popper: A tool for releasing air bubbles and adjusting headspace by running along the inside of the jar. Ensure it's made of non-reactive materials, such as plastic or wood, to avoid affecting the acidity of the food.

SAFETY GUIDELINES

Ensuring safety during the waterbath canning process is crucial to prevent foodborne illnesses and to preserve the quality of the canned goods. By following these safety guidelines, you can enhance the success of your waterbath canning endeavors while prioritizing the safety and well-being of those who consume the preserved foods. Here are important safety guidelines to follow:

Start with Clean and Sterile Equipment: Properly sterilized equipment minimizes the risk of contamination. Wash all equipment, including jars, lids, bands, and utensils, in hot, soapy water. Sterilize jars and lids by boiling them in water for 10 minutes or using a dishwasher's sterilize cycle. Keep all work surfaces clean and sanitized.

Use Reliable and Tested Recipes: Following tested recipes ensures the correct acidity and processing times for safe canning. Use recipes from reputable sources, such as extension services, trusted cookbooks, or official canning guides. Do not alter ingredient proportions or substitute ingredients without consulting a reliable source.

Maintain Proper Acid Levels: High-acid foods are suitable for waterbath canning. The acidity helps inhibit the growth of harmful microorganisms. For fruits with low acidity, such as tomatoes, add citric acid or lemon juice to achieve the recommended pH level. Do not reduce the amount of acid specified in a recipe.

Follow Headspace Recommendations: Maintaining the correct headspace allows for proper expansion during processing and helps create a reliable seal. Use a headspace tool to measure and maintain the specified headspace for each recipe.

Do not overfill jars; leave the recommended space at the top.

Ensure Proper Jar Sealing: A proper seal is critical for preventing spoilage and ensuring food safety. Use new, undamaged lids for each canning session. Tighten bands until resistance is felt, and then adjust to fingertip tight (do not over-tighten).

Process Jars for the Correct Time and Temperature: Inadequate processing can result in under-pasteurized food, increasing the risk of spoilage and foodborne illness. Follow the recommended processing time specified in the recipe. Ensure the water in the canner covers the jars by at least 1 to 2 inches.

Cool Jars Properly: Gradual cooling helps form a strong vacuum seal and reduces the risk of jar breakage. After processing, turn off the heat and let jars sit in the water for 5 minutes before removing them. Allow jars to cool on a clean towel or cooling rack, leaving space between jars to promote air circulation.

Check Seals and Store Properly: Properly sealed jars are a sign of successful canning, and correct storage conditions are essential for long-term preservation. Check seals by pressing down on the center of each lid; it should not flex or make a popping sound. Store jars in a cool, dark, and dry place.

Discard Unsealed Jars or Spoiled Food: Unsealed jars or spoiled food may pose health risks. Discard any jars with a compromised seal or signs of spoilage, such as off-putting odors, discoloration, or unusual textures.

Label Jars with Date and Contents: Keeping track of when the food was canned ensures that you consume it within its optimal period. Clearly label each jar with the date of canning and the contents.

WATERBATH CANNING RECIPES

Classic Strawberry Jam

Ingredients:

- 4 cups fresh strawberries, hulled and crushed
- 5 cups granulated sugar
- 1/4 cup fresh lemon juice
- 1 package (1.75 oz) fruit pectin
- Butter (optional, for reducing foaming)

Instructions:

1. Prepare Jars and Lids: Wash canning jars, lids, and bands in hot, soapy water. Sterilize the jars by boiling them for 10 minutes or using the sterilize cycle in a dishwasher. Keep lids in warm water to soften the sealing compound.

2. Prepare Strawberries: Hull the strawberries and crush them using a potato masher or food processor, leaving some small chunks for texture. Measure 4 cups of crushed strawberries and place them in a large, heavy-bottomed pot.

3. Add Lemon Juice and Pectin: Stir in fresh lemon juice to enhance flavor and provide natural pectin. This helps the jam set properly. Gradually whisk in the fruit pectin, ensuring it is well-distributed to avoid clumping.

4. Bring to a Boil: Over medium-high heat, bring the strawberry mixture to a full rolling boil, stirring constantly. Once boiling, add the granulated sugar all at once, continuing to stir.

5. Boil and Stir: Return the mixture to a rapid boil and stir constantly to prevent scorching. If foaming occurs, add a small amount of butter (1/2 teaspoon) to reduce foaming.

6. Check for Gel Stage: Test for gel stage by placing a small spoonful of the hot jam on a cold plate and letting it sit for a minute. Run your finger through it; if it wrinkles, it has reached the gel stage.

7. Skim off Foam: Skim off any foam that has formed on the surface of the jam using a spoon.

8. Fill Jars: Ladle the hot jam into prepared, hot jars, leaving a 1/4-inch headspace.

Wipe the rims of the jars with a clean, damp cloth to remove any residue.

9. Apply Lids and Bands: Place lids on the jars and screw bands on fingertip-tight. Do not over-tighten.

10. Process in Waterbath Canner: - Process the jars in a boiling waterbath canner for 10 minutes, ensuring the water covers the jars by at least 1 to 2 inches.

11. Cool and Check Seals: - After processing, turn off the heat and let jars sit in the water for 5 minutes. Remove jars and let them cool on a clean towel or cooling rack. - Once cooled, check the seals by pressing down on the center of each lid. A proper seal should not flex or make a popping sound.

12. Label and Store: - Label each jar with the date and contents. - Store in a cool, dark, and dry place.

Enjoy the classic goodness of homemade strawberry jam on toast, in desserts, or as a delightful gift for friends and family.

Peach Preserves

Ingredients:

- 6 cups ripe peaches, peeled, pitted, and chopped
- 4 cups granulated sugar
- 1/4 cup fresh lemon juice
- 1/4 cup bourbon
- 1 teaspoon vanilla extract
- 1/2 teaspoon ground cinnamon
- 1 package (1.75 oz) fruit pectin

Instructions:

1. Prepare Jars and Lids: Wash canning jars, lids, and bands in hot, soapy water. Sterilize the jars by boiling them for 10 minutes or using the sterilize cycle in a dishwasher. Keep lids in warm water to soften the sealing compound.

2. Prepare Peaches: Peel, pit, and chop the ripe peaches. Measure 6 cups of chopped peaches and place them in a large, heavy-bottomed pot.

3. Add Lemon Juice and Bourbon: Stir in fresh lemon juice to enhance flavor and acidity. Add bourbon for depth of flavor. Adjust the amount based on personal preference or omit for a non-alcoholic version.

4. Mix in Sugar and Pectin: Gradually add granulated sugar, stirring to combine. Allow the peaches to macerate in the sugar for about 10-15 minutes. Gradually whisk in the fruit pectin, ensuring it is well-distributed to avoid clumping.

5. Bring to a Boil: Over medium-high heat, bring the peach mixture to a full rolling boil, stirring constantly. Once boiling, continue to stir and boil for 1-2 minutes to dissolve the sugar.

6. Add Vanilla and Cinnamon: Stir in vanilla extract and ground cinnamon, adding warmth and enhancing the overall flavor profile.

7. Check for Gel Stage: Test for gel stage by placing a small spoonful of the hot preserves on a cold plate. Let it sit for a minute and run your finger through it. If it wrinkles, it has reached the gel stage.

8. Fill Jars: Ladle the hot peach preserves into prepared, hot jars, leaving a 1/4-inch headspace. Wipe the rims of the jars with a clean, damp cloth to remove any residue.

9. Apply Lids and Bands: Place lids on the jars and screw bands on fingertip-tight. Do not over-tighten.

10. Process in Waterbath Canner: - Process the jars in a boiling waterbath canner for 10 minutes, ensuring the water covers the jars by at least 1 to 2 inches.

11. Cool and Check Seals: - After processing, turn off the heat and let jars sit in the water for 5 minutes. Remove jars and let them cool on a clean towel or cooling rack. Once cooled, check the seals by pressing down on the center of each lid. A proper seal should not flex or make a popping sound.

12. Label and Store: - Label each jar with the date and contents. - Store in a cool, dark, and dry place.

Enjoy your Peach Bourbon Preserves! Ideal for spreading on toast, topping desserts, or serving alongside cheese and crackers. The addition of bourbon adds a sophisticated twist to this classic preserve.

Blueberry Compote

Ingredients:

- 6 cups fresh blueberries
- 2 cups granulated sugar
- 1/4 cup fresh lemon juice
- Zest of one lemon
- 1/2 teaspoon ground cinnamon
- 1/4 teaspoon nutmeg (optional, for a hint of warmth)

Instructions:

1. Prepare Jars and Lids: Wash canning jars, lids, and bands in hot, soapy water. Sterilize the jars by boiling them for 10 minutes or using the sterilize cycle in a dishwasher. Keep lids in warm water to soften the sealing compound.

2. Prepare Blueberries: Wash and gently pat dry the fresh blueberries. Measure 6 cups of blueberries and place them in a large, heavy-bottomed pot.

3. Add Sugar and Lemon: Pour granulated sugar over the blueberries and add fresh lemon juice and lemon zest. Stir the mixture gently to combine, allowing the sugar to dissolve.

4. Bring to a Simmer: Over medium heat, bring the blueberry mixture to a gentle simmer, stirring occasionally. Continue simmering for 10-15 minutes until the blueberries release their juices and the mixture thickens slightly.

5. Add Spices: Stir in ground cinnamon and nutmeg (if using) for added depth of flavor. Adjust the spices based on personal preference.

6. Check Consistency: To check for desired consistency, place a small spoonful of the compote on a cold plate. Allow it to cool for a minute; if it thickens to your liking, it's ready.

7. Fill Jars: Ladle the hot blueberry compote into prepared, hot jars, leaving a 1/4-inch headspace. Wipe the rims of the jars with a clean, damp cloth to remove any residue.

8. Apply Lids and Bands: Place lids on the jars and screw bands on fingertip-tight. Do not over-tighten.

9. Process in Waterbath Canner: - Process the jars in a boiling waterbath canner for 10 minutes, ensuring the water covers the jars by at least 1 to 2 inches.

10. Cool and Check Seals: - After processing, turn off the heat and let jars sit in the water for 5 minutes. Remove jars and let them cool on a clean towel or cooling rack. Once cooled, check the seals by pressing down on the center of each lid. A proper seal should not flex or make a popping sound.

11. Label and Store: Label each jar with the date and contents. Store in a cool, dark, and dry place.

Serve the Blueberry Compote: This versatile compote can be enjoyed on pancakes, waffles, ice cream, yogurt, or as a topping for desserts. Its vibrant flavor captures the essence of fresh blueberries, making it a delightful addition to your pantry.

Raspberry-Lime Jam:

Ingredients:

- 5 cups fresh raspberries
- 4 cups granulated sugar
- Zest and juice of two limes
- 1 package (1.75 oz) fruit pectin

Instructions:

1. Combine raspberries, sugar, lime zest, and lime juice in a pot.
2. Bring the mixture to a boil, stirring constantly.
3. Stir in the fruit pectin and boil for an additional 1-2 minutes.
4. Follow the standard waterbath canning process.

Vanilla-Spiced Pear Butter:

Ingredients:

- 8 cups ripe pears, peeled, cored, and chopped
- 2 cups brown sugar
- 1 vanilla bean, split and scraped
- 1 teaspoon ground cinnamon
- 1/2 teaspoon ground nutmeg

- 1/4 teaspoon cloves

Instructions:

1. Cook pears, brown sugar, and vanilla in a pot until softened.
2. Puree the mixture and return it to the pot.
3. Add spices and simmer until thickened.
4. Waterbath can the pear butter in sterilized jars.

Cherry-Basil Preserves:

Ingredients:

- 6 cups fresh cherries, pitted and halved
- 4 cups granulated sugar
- 1/4 cup fresh lemon juice
- 1/4 cup fresh basil, finely chopped
- 1 package (1.75 oz) fruit pectin

Instructions:

1. Combine cherries, sugar, lemon juice, and basil in a pot.
2. Bring the mixture to a rapid boil, stirring frequently.
3. Stir in the fruit pectin and boil for an additional 1-2 minutes.
4. Follow the standard waterbath canning process.

Mango-Peach Salsa:

Ingredients:

- 4 cups ripe mango, peeled and diced
- 2 cups ripe peaches, peeled and diced
- 1 cup red bell pepper, diced
- 1/2 cup red onion, finely chopped
- 1/4 cup fresh cilantro, chopped
- 1/4 cup fresh lime juice
- 1 teaspoon cumin
- 1/2 teaspoon chili powder

Instructions:

1. Combine all ingredients in a pot and bring to a simmer.
2. Simmer for 5-7 minutes until flavors meld.
3. Ladle the salsa into hot, sterilized jars and waterbath can.

Gingered Pineapple Jam:

Ingredients:

- 5 cups fresh pineapple, finely chopped
- 4 cups granulated sugar
- 1/4 cup fresh lemon juice
- 2 tablespoons fresh ginger, grated
- 1 package (1.75 oz) fruit pectin

Instructions:

1. Combine pineapple, sugar, lemon juice, and ginger in a pot.
2. Bring the mixture to a boil, stirring constantly.
3. Stir in the fruit pectin and boil for an additional 1-2 minutes.
4. Follow the standard waterbath canning process.

Enjoy experimenting with these flavorful fruit recipes! They're perfect for adding variety to your pantry and making delightful homemade gifts.

Pickled Cucumbers:

Ingredients:

- 6 cups pickling cucumbers, sliced
- 2 cups white vinegar
- 2 cups water
- 1/4 cup pickling salt
- 2 tablespoons sugar
- 4 cloves garlic, peeled
- 2 teaspoons dill seeds
- 1 teaspoon black peppercorns
- 1 teaspoon mustard seeds

Instructions:

1. In a saucepan, combine vinegar, water, pickling salt, and sugar. Bring to a boil, stirring to dissolve the salt and sugar.

2. Pack cucumber slices into sterilized jars, adding garlic cloves, dill seeds, black peppercorns, and mustard seeds to each jar.

3. Pour the hot brine over the cucumbers, leaving a 1/2-inch headspace.

4. Remove air bubbles, wipe jar rims, and apply lids.

5. Process in a waterbath canner for 10 minutes.

6. Allow the pickles to cool and develop flavor for a few weeks before enjoying.

Salsa Verde

Ingredients:

- 8 cups tomatillos, husked and chopped
- 1 cup green bell peppers, chopped
- 1 cup onion, chopped
- 1 cup green chili peppers, chopped
- 4 cloves garlic, minced
- 1 cup cilantro, chopped
- 1 cup white vinegar
- 1 tablespoon pickling salt
- 1 teaspoon cumin

Instructions:

1. Combine tomatillos, bell peppers, onion, green chili peppers, and garlic in a large pot.
2. Add vinegar, pickling salt, and cumin. Bring the mixture to a boil, then simmer for 10 minutes.
3. Stir in cilantro and continue to simmer for an additional 5 minutes.
4. Ladle the hot salsa into sterilized jars, leaving a 1/2-inch headspace.
5. Remove air bubbles, wipe jar rims, and apply lids.
6. Process in a waterbath canner for 15 minutes.
7. Allow the salsa to cool before storing. The flavors will intensify over time.

Roasted Tomato Sauce:

Ingredients:

- 10 cups tomatoes, peeled, seeded, and chopped
- 2 cups onions, chopped
- 1 cup bell peppers, chopped
- 4 cloves garlic, minced
- 1/4 cup olive oil
- 2 teaspoons dried oregano
- 2 teaspoons dried basil
- 1 teaspoon salt
- 1/2 teaspoon black pepper

Instructions:

1. Preheat the oven to 400°F (200°C).
2. Toss tomatoes, onions, bell peppers, and garlic with olive oil, oregano, basil, salt, and black pepper.
3. Spread the mixture on baking sheets and roast in the oven for 45-60 minutes, stirring occasionally.
4. Allow the roasted vegetables to cool slightly, then puree in a blender or food processor until smooth.
5. Transfer the sauce to a large pot and bring it to a simmer.
6. Ladle the hot sauce into sterilized jars, leaving a 1/2-inch headspace.
7. Remove air bubbles, wipe jar rims, and apply lids.
8. Process in a waterbath canner for 35 minutes.
9. Allow the tomato sauce to cool before storing. Use it in various dishes like pasta, pizzas, or casseroles.

Dilly Beans

Ingredients:

- 4 cups fresh green beans, trimmed
- 2 cups white vinegar
- 2 cups water
- 1/4 cup pickling salt
- 4 cloves garlic, peeled
- 4 teaspoons dill seeds
- 2 teaspoons red pepper flakes (optional, for heat)

Instructions:

1. In a saucepan, combine vinegar, water, pickling salt, and, if desired, red pepper flakes. Bring to a boil.
2. Pack the trimmed green beans into sterilized jars, adding a garlic clove and 1 teaspoon of dill seeds to each jar.
3. Pour the hot brine over the green beans, leaving a 1/2-inch headspace.
4. Remove air bubbles, wipe jar rims, and apply lids.
5. Process in a waterbath canner for 10 minutes.
6. Allow the dilly beans to sit for a few weeks for optimal flavor development.

Mixed Vegetable Medley Relish

Ingredients:

- 2 cups cauliflower florets
- 2 cups carrots, diced
- 2 cups red bell peppers, diced
- 1 cup green bell peppers, diced
- 1 cup celery, diced
- 1 cup onions, finely chopped
- 3 cups white vinegar
- 2 cups granulated sugar
- 1 tablespoon mustard seeds
- 1 tablespoon celery seeds
- 1 teaspoon turmeric

- 1/2 teaspoon red pepper flakes (optional, for heat)

Instructions:

1. Combine cauliflower, carrots, red and green bell peppers, celery, and onions in a large pot.
2. In a separate saucepan, mix vinegar, sugar, mustard seeds, celery seeds, turmeric, and, if desired, red pepper flakes. Bring to a boil.
3. Pour the hot liquid over the vegetable mixture and bring to a gentle boil.
4. Simmer for 10-15 minutes until the vegetables are tender-crisp.
5. Ladle the hot relish into sterilized jars, leaving a 1/2-inch headspace.
6. Remove air bubbles, wipe jar rims, and apply lids.
7. Process in a waterbath canner for 15 minutes.
8. Allow the mixed vegetable medley relish to cool before storing. It's a versatile condiment for sandwiches, salads, or as a side dish.

Raspberry Jam:

Ingredients:

- 6 cups fresh raspberries
- 5 cups granulated sugar
- 1/4 cup fresh lemon juice
- 1 package (1.75 oz) fruit pectin

Instructions:

1. Crush raspberries in a large, heavy-bottomed pot using a potato masher.

2. Add sugar and lemon juice to the crushed raspberries, stirring well.

3. Bring the mixture to a boil over medium-high heat, stirring constantly.

4. Stir in the fruit pectin and boil for an additional 1-2 minutes.

5. Ladle the hot jam into sterilized jars, leaving a 1/4-inch headspace.

6. Remove air bubbles, wipe jar rims, and apply lids.

7. Process in a waterbath canner for 10 minutes.

8. Allow the raspberry jam to cool before storing. Enjoy on toast, in desserts, or as a flavorful topping.

Orange Marmalade:

Ingredients:

- 4 cups oranges, thinly sliced and chopped
- 2 lemons, thinly sliced and chopped
- 8 cups water
- 8 cups granulated sugar
- 1 package (1.75 oz) fruit pectin

Instructions:

1. Combine oranges, lemons, and water in a large pot. Bring to a boil and simmer for 10 minutes.

2. Add sugar to the fruit mixture, stirring until dissolved.

3. Bring the mixture to a rapid boil, then stir in the fruit pectin.

4. Boil for an additional 1-2 minutes, stirring constantly.

5. Ladle the hot marmalade into sterilized jars, leaving a 1/4-inch headspace.

6. Remove air bubbles, wipe jar rims, and apply lids.

7. Process in a waterbath canner for 10 minutes.

8. Allow the orange marmalade to cool and set before storing. Spread it on toast or use it as a glaze for meats.

Apple Butter:

Ingredients:

- 6 lbs apples, peeled, cored, and chopped
- 2 cups granulated sugar
- 2 teaspoons ground cinnamon
- 1/2 teaspoon ground cloves
- 1/2 teaspoon ground nutmeg
- 1/4 teaspoon salt

Instructions:

1. Place chopped apples in a slow cooker and cook on low for 8-10 hours or until the apples are soft.

2. Puree the cooked apples using an immersion blender or food processor until smooth.

3. Transfer the apple puree to a large pot, add sugar, cinnamon, cloves, nutmeg, and salt. Stir well.

4. Cook the mixture over low heat, stirring frequently, until it thickens to the desired consistency.

5. Ladle the hot apple butter into sterilized jars, leaving a 1/4-inch headspace.

6. Remove air bubbles, wipe jar rims, and apply lids.

7. Process in a waterbath canner for 10 minutes.

8. Allow the apple butter to cool before storing. Spread it on bread, pancakes, or use it in baking for a rich apple flavor.

Mango Chutney

Ingredients:

- 6 cups ripe mango, peeled and diced
- 2 cups red bell pepper, finely chopped
- 1 cup onion, finely chopped
- 1 cup raisins
- 2 cups brown sugar
- 2 cups apple cider vinegar
- 1 tablespoon fresh ginger, grated
- 1 teaspoon mustard seeds
- 1 teaspoon ground cinnamon
- 1/2 teaspoon ground cloves

Instructions:

1. Combine mango, red bell pepper, onion, raisins, brown sugar, apple cider vinegar, ginger, mustard seeds, cinnamon, and cloves in a large pot.

2. Bring the mixture to a boil, then reduce heat and simmer until the chutney thickens and the flavors meld (approximately 45-60 minutes).

3. Ladle the hot mango chutney into sterilized jars, leaving a 1/2-inch headspace.

4. Remove air bubbles, wipe jar rims, and apply lids.

5. Process in a waterbath canner for 15 minutes.

6. Allow the mango chutney to cool before storing. It pairs wonderfully with grilled meats, curries, or cheese.

Bread and Butter Pickles

Ingredients:

- 5 cups cucumbers, thinly sliced
- 2 cups onions, thinly sliced
- 1/4 cup pickling salt
- 2 cups white vinegar
- 2 cups granulated sugar
- 1 tablespoon mustard seeds
- 1 teaspoon ground turmeric
- 1 teaspoon celery seeds

Instructions:

1. Combine cucumber and onion slices in a large bowl, sprinkle with pickling salt, and cover with ice. Let it stand for 1-2 hours.

2. Rinse and drain the cucumber and onion mixture thoroughly.

3. In a pot, combine white vinegar, sugar, mustard seeds, turmeric, and celery seeds. Bring to a boil.

4. Add the cucumber and onion slices to the boiling liquid and return to a boil, stirring gently.

5. Ladle the hot pickles into sterilized jars, leaving a 1/2-inch headspace.

6. Remove air bubbles, wipe jar rims, and apply lids.

7. Process in a waterbath canner for 10 minutes.

8. Allow the bread and butter pickles to cool before storing. Enjoy them as a crunchy, sweet addition to sandwiches or salads.

Spiced Peach Chutney:

Ingredients:

- 6 cups peaches, peeled and chopped
- 2 cups red bell pepper, finely chopped
- 1 cup onion, finely chopped
- 1 cup raisins
- 2 cups brown sugar
- 2 cups apple cider vinegar
- 1 tablespoon fresh ginger, grated
- 1 teaspoon mustard seeds
- 1 teaspoon ground cinnamon
- 1/2 teaspoon ground cloves
- 1/2 teaspoon red pepper flakes (optional, for heat)

Instructions:

1. Combine peaches, red bell pepper, onion, raisins, brown sugar, apple cider vinegar, ginger, mustard seeds, cinnamon, cloves, and red pepper flakes (if using) in a large pot.

2. Bring the mixture to a boil, then reduce heat and simmer until the chutney thickens and the flavors meld (approximately 45-60 minutes).

3. Ladle the hot spiced peach chutney into sterilized jars, leaving a 1/2-inch headspace.

4. Remove air bubbles, wipe jar rims, and apply lids.

5. Process in a waterbath canner for 15 minutes.

6. Allow the spiced peach chutney to cool before storing. It's a versatile condiment that pairs well with grilled meats, cheese, or as a topping for crackers.

Zesty Tomato Relish:

Ingredients:

- 8 cups tomatoes, finely chopped
- 2 cups onions, finely chopped
- 1 cup red bell pepper, finely chopped
- 1 cup green bell pepper, finely chopped
- 2 cups apple cider vinegar
- 2 cups granulated sugar
- 1 tablespoon mustard seeds
- 1 teaspoon celery seeds
- 1 teaspoon ground turmeric

- 1 teaspoon salt
- 1/2 teaspoon black pepper

Instructions:

1. Combine tomatoes, onions, red and green bell peppers, apple cider vinegar, sugar, mustard seeds, celery seeds, turmeric, salt, and black pepper in a large pot.
2. Bring the mixture to a boil, then simmer over medium heat until the relish thickens and vegetables are tender (approximately 45-60 minutes).
3. Ladle the hot zesty tomato relish into sterilized jars, leaving a 1/2-inch headspace.
4. Remove air bubbles, wipe jar rims, and apply lids.
5. Process in a waterbath canner for 15 minutes.
6. Allow the zesty tomato relish to cool before storing. It's a delightful accompaniment to burgers, hot dogs, or as a topping for grilled vegetables.

Cranberry Orange Relish:

Ingredients:

- 4 cups cranberries, fresh or frozen
- 2 large oranges, peeled and segmented
- 2 cups granulated sugar
- 1/2 cup orange juice
- Zest of one orange
- 1/2 cup pecans, chopped (optional)

Instructions:

1. In a food processor, combine cranberries and orange segments. Pulse until coarsely chopped.
2. Transfer the mixture to a pot and add granulated sugar, orange juice, and orange zest.
3. Bring the relish to a simmer over medium heat, stirring occasionally, until the cranberries burst and the mixture thickens (approximately 15-20 minutes).
4. Stir in chopped pecans if desired.
5. Ladle the hot cranberry orange relish into sterilized jars, leaving a 1/2-inch headspace.
6. Remove air bubbles, wipe jar rims, and apply lids.
7. Process in a waterbath canner for 15 minutes.
8. Allow the cranberry orange relish to cool before storing. It's a vibrant and tangy addition to Thanksgiving dinners or as a festive spread.

Sweet and Spicy Bread and Butter Pickles:

Ingredients:

- 5 cups cucumbers, thinly sliced
- 2 cups onions, thinly sliced
- 1/4 cup pickling salt
- 2 cups white vinegar
- 2 cups granulated sugar

- 1 tablespoon mustard seeds
- 1 teaspoon celery seeds
- 1 teaspoon turmeric
- 1 teaspoon red pepper flakes
- 1/2 teaspoon black peppercorns

Instructions:

1. Combine cucumber and onion slices in a large bowl, sprinkle with pickling salt, and cover with ice. Let it stand for 1-2 hours.
2. Rinse and drain the cucumber and onion mixture thoroughly.
3. In a pot, combine white vinegar, sugar, mustard seeds, celery seeds, turmeric, red pepper flakes, and black peppercorns. Bring to a boil.
4. Add the cucumber and onion slices to the boiling liquid and return to a boil, stirring gently.
5. Ladle the hot pickles into sterilized jars, leaving a 1/2-inch headspace.
6. Remove air bubbles, wipe jar rims, and apply lids.
7. Process in a waterbath canner for 10 minutes.
8. Allow the sweet and spicy bread and butter pickles to cool before storing. Enjoy them as a delightful addition to sandwiches, burgers, or charcuterie boards.

Pineapple Mango Salsa

Ingredients:

- 3 cups pineapple, diced

- 2 cups mango, diced
- 1 cup red onion, finely chopped
- 1 cup red bell pepper, finely chopped
- 1/2 cup fresh cilantro, chopped
- 1/4 cup jalapeño, minced (adjust to taste)
- 1/4 cup lime juice
- 1 teaspoon ground cumin
- Salt and pepper to taste

Instructions:

1. In a large bowl, combine pineapple, mango, red onion, red bell pepper, cilantro, and jalapeño.
2. In a separate bowl, mix lime juice and ground cumin. Pour over the fruit mixture and toss gently to combine.
3. Season with salt and pepper to taste.
4. Ladle the fresh pineapple mango salsa into sterilized jars, leaving a 1/2-inch headspace.
5. Remove air bubbles, wipe jar rims, and apply lids.
6. Process in a waterbath canner for 10 minutes.
7. Allow the pineapple mango salsa to cool before storing. Serve it with tortilla chips, grilled chicken, or fish.

Blueberry-Lemon Jam:

Ingredients:

- 6 cups fresh blueberries
- 5 cups granulated sugar
- 1/4 cup fresh lemon juice
- Zest of two lemons
- 1 package (1.75 oz) fruit pectin

Instructions:

1) Crush blueberries in a large pot.
2) Add sugar, lemon juice, and lemon zest, stirring well.
3) Bring the mixture to a boil over medium-high heat, stirring constantly.
4) Stir in the fruit pectin and boil for an additional 1-2 minutes.
5) Ladle the hot blueberry-lemon jam into sterilized jars, leaving a 1/4-inch headspace.
6) Process in a waterbath canner for 10 minutes.
7) Allow the jam to cool before storing. Spread it on toast or use it in pastries.

Strawberry-Rhubarb Preserves:

Ingredients:

- 6 cups fresh strawberries, hulled and halved
- 4 cups rhubarb, chopped
- 4 cups granulated sugar

- 1/4 cup fresh lemon juice
- 1 package (1.75 oz) fruit pectin

Instructions:

1) Combine strawberries, rhubarb, sugar, and lemon juice in a pot.
2) Bring the mixture to a boil, then simmer until the fruit is soft.
3) Stir in the fruit pectin and boil for an additional 1-2 minutes.
4) Ladle the hot strawberry-rhubarb preserves into sterilized jars, leaving a 1/4-inch headspace.
5) Process in a waterbath canner for 10 minutes.
6) Allow the preserves to cool before storing. Enjoy on scones or as a dessert topping.

Blackberry Sage Jelly:

Ingredients:

- 5 cups blackberries
- 4 cups granulated sugar
- 1/4 cup fresh sage leaves, chopped
- 1/4 cup fresh lemon juice
- 1 package (1.75 oz) fruit pectin

Instructions:

1) Crush blackberries in a large pot and add sugar and sage.

2) Bring the mixture to a boil, then simmer for 10 minutes.

3) Strain the juice through a fine mesh sieve or cheesecloth.

4) Return the juice to the pot, add lemon juice, and bring to a boil.

5) Stir in the fruit pectin and boil for an additional 1-2 minutes.

6) Ladle the hot blackberry sage jelly into sterilized jars, leaving a 1/4-inch headspace.

7) Process in a waterbath canner for 10 minutes.

8) Allow the jelly to cool before storing. Serve with cheese or as a glaze for meats.

Caramelized Onion and Fig Chutney:

Ingredients:

- 4 cups red onions, thinly sliced
- 2 cups dried figs, chopped
- 2 cups brown sugar
- 2 cups apple cider vinegar
- 1 cup raisins
- 1 tablespoon fresh ginger, grated
- 1 teaspoon mustard seeds
- 1 teaspoon ground cinnamon
- 1/2 teaspoon ground cloves

Instructions:

1) Caramelize red onions in a pot over low heat.

2) Add figs, brown sugar, apple cider vinegar, raisins, ginger, mustard seeds, cinnamon, and cloves.

3) Bring the mixture to a boil, then simmer until thickened.

4) Ladle the hot onion and fig chutney into sterilized jars, leaving a 1/2-inch headspace.

5) Process in a waterbath canner for 15 minutes.

6) Allow the chutney to cool before storing. Pair it with grilled meats or as a topping for sandwiches.

Corn and Black Bean Salsa:

Ingredients:

- 4 cups corn kernels (fresh or frozen)
- 2 cups black beans, cooked and drained
- 1 cup red onion, finely chopped
- 1 cup red bell pepper, finely chopped
- 1/2 cup cilantro, chopped
- 1/4 cup jalapeño, minced (adjust to taste)
- 1/4 cup lime juice
- 1 teaspoon ground cumin
- Salt and pepper to taste

Instructions:

1) In a large bowl, combine corn, black beans, red onion, red bell pepper, cilantro, and jalapeño.

2) In a separate bowl, mix lime juice and ground cumin. Pour over the corn and bean mixture and toss gently to combine.

3) Season with salt and pepper to taste.

4) Ladle the corn and black bean salsa into sterilized jars, leaving a 1/2-inch headspace.

5) Process in a waterbath canner for 10 minutes.

6) Allow the salsa to cool before storing. Serve it with tortilla chips or as a topping for grilled chicken.

Garlic-Dill Pickled Asparagus:

Ingredients:

- 4 cups asparagus spears, trimmed
- 4 cloves garlic, peeled
- 2 cups white vinegar
- 2 cups water
- 2 tablespoons pickling salt
- 2 teaspoons dill seeds
- 1 teaspoon black peppercorns

Instructions:

1) Blanch asparagus spears in boiling water for 2 minutes, then transfer to an ice bath.

2) Pack asparagus spears and garlic cloves into sterilized jars.

3) In a saucepan, combine white vinegar, water, pickling salt, dill seeds, and black peppercorns. Bring to a boil.

4) Pour the hot brine over the asparagus, leaving a 1/2-inch headspace.

5) Remove air bubbles, wipe jar rims, and apply lids.

6) Process in a waterbath canner for 10 minutes.

7) Allow the pickled asparagus to cool before storing. Enjoy as a tangy and crisp side dish or appetizer.

Cherry Amaretto Jam:

Ingredients:

6 cups fresh cherries, pitted and chopped

5 cups granulated sugar

1/4 cup amaretto liqueur

1/4 cup fresh lemon juice

1 package (1.75 oz) fruit pectin

Instructions:

1) Combine cherries, sugar, amaretto, and lemon juice in a pot.

2) Bring the mixture to a boil, then simmer until the cherries are soft.

3) Stir in the fruit pectin and boil for an additional 1-2 minutes.

4) Ladle the hot cherry amaretto jam into sterilized jars, leaving a 1/4-inch headspace.

5) Process in a waterbath canner for 10 minutes.

6) Allow the jam to cool before storing. Spread it on toast or use it in desserts.

Spicy Pineapple Habanero Relish:

Ingredients:

- 4 cups pineapple, diced
- 2 cups red bell pepper, finely chopped
- 1 cup red onion, finely chopped
- 2 habanero peppers, minced (seeds removed for less heat)
- 2 cups white vinegar
- 2 cups granulated sugar
- 1 teaspoon ground cumin
- 1 teaspoon ground coriander
- 1/2 teaspoon turmeric

Instructions:

1) Combine pineapple, red bell pepper, red onion, habanero peppers, white vinegar, sugar, cumin, coriander, and turmeric in a pot.
2) Bring the mixture to a boil, then simmer until the relish thickens.
3) Ladle the hot pineapple habanero relish into sterilized jars, leaving a 1/2-inch headspace.
4) Process in a waterbath canner for 15 minutes.
5) Allow the relish to cool before storing. Use it as a spicy condiment for grilled meats or tacos.

Apricot Rosemary Preserves:

Ingredients:

- 6 cups fresh apricots, pitted and chopped
- 4 cups granulated sugar
- 1/4 cup fresh lemon juice
- 2 tablespoons fresh rosemary, finely chopped
- 1 package (1.75 oz) fruit pectin

Instructions:

1) Combine apricots, sugar, lemon juice, and rosemary in a pot.
2) Bring the mixture to a boil, then simmer until the apricots are tender.
3) Stir in the fruit pectin and boil for an additional 1-2 minutes.
4) Ladle the hot apricot rosemary preserves into sterilized jars, leaving a 1/4-inch headspace.
5) Process in a waterbath canner for 10 minutes.
6) Allow the preserves to cool before storing. Enjoy the unique flavor combination on toast or with cheese.

Mango Avocado Salsa:

Ingredients:

- 3 cups mango, diced
- 2 avocados, diced
- 1 cup red onion, finely chopped

- 1 cup cilantro, chopped
- 1/4 cup jalapeño, minced
- 1/4 cup lime juice
- 1 teaspoon ground cumin
- Salt and pepper to taste

Instructions:

1) In a large bowl, combine mango, avocados, red onion, cilantro, and jalapeño.
2) In a separate bowl, mix lime juice and ground cumin. Pour over the mango and avocado mixture and toss gently to combine.
3) Season with salt and pepper to taste.
4) Ladle the mango avocado salsa into sterilized jars, leaving a 1/2-inch headspace.
5) Process in a waterbath canner for 10 minutes.
6) Allow the salsa to cool before storing. Serve it with grilled fish, chicken, or as a refreshing dip.

Spicy Garlic Dill Pickles:

Ingredients:

- 5 cups pickling cucumbers, sliced
- 4 cloves garlic, peeled
- 2 cups white vinegar
- 2 cups water
- 2 tablespoons pickling salt

- 1 tablespoon dill seeds
- 1 tablespoon red pepper flakes

Instructions:

1) Pack cucumber slices and garlic cloves into sterilized jars.
2) In a saucepan, combine white vinegar, water, pickling salt, dill seeds, and red pepper flakes. Bring to a boil.
3) Pour the hot brine over the cucumbers, leaving a 1/2-inch headspace.
4) Remove air bubbles, wipe jar rims, and apply lids.
5) Process in a waterbath canner for 10 minutes.
6) Allow the spicy garlic dill pickles to cool before storing. Enjoy the heat and crunch as a snack or alongside sandwiches.

Pomegranate Jelly:

Ingredients:

- 5 cups pomegranate juice (freshly squeezed or store-bought)
- 7 cups granulated sugar
- 1/4 cup fresh lemon juice
- 1 package (1.75 oz) fruit pectin

Instructions:

1) In a large pot, combine pomegranate juice, sugar, and lemon juice.
2) Bring the mixture to a boil, stirring constantly.

3) Stir in the fruit pectin and boil for an additional 1-2 minutes.

4) Ladle the hot pomegranate jelly into sterilized jars, leaving a 1/4-inch headspace.

5) Process in a waterbath canner for 10 minutes.

6) Allow the jelly to cool before storing. Spread it on toast, use it as a glaze, or mix it into sauces.

TROUBLESHOOTING COMMON ISSUES IN WATERBATH CANNING:

1. Inconsistent Seal or Failure to Seal:

Cause: Jar rims not properly cleaned, lids not applied correctly, or lids not sitting flat.

Solution: Ensure jar rims are clean, lids are placed on jars with even pressure, and bands are tightened fingertip-tight. Check for any nicks on jar rims.

2. Jars Leaking During Processing:

Cause: Over-tightening lids or using defective lids.

Solution: Apply lids fingertip-tight; avoid over-tightening. Check for lid defects or use new lids.

3. Floating Food in Jars:

Cause: Air trapped during filling, food not packed tightly, or too much headspace.

Solution: Pack food tightly, remove air bubbles using a non-metallic spatula, and maintain recommended headspace.

4. Discoloration or Darkening of Food:

Cause: Oxidation due to exposure to air or inadequate processing time.

Solution: Fill jars quickly, remove air bubbles, and ensure proper processing times. Use approved recipes.

5. Mold Growth on Jar Lid or Food Surface:

Cause: Contamination during the canning process or improper storage.

Solution: Use proper canning techniques, sterilize jars, lids, and utensils. Store jars in a cool, dark, and dry place.

6. Liquid Loss During Processing:

Cause: Evaporation during processing or improper headspace.

Solution: Ensure proper headspace as per the recipe. Maintain a gentle simmer during processing, not a vigorous boil.

7. Siphoning (Liquid Loss Between Jar and Lid):

Cause: Rapid temperature changes during cooling, over-tightening lids, or insufficient headspace.

Solution: Allow jars to cool naturally, tighten lids fingertip-tight, and maintain recommended headspace.

8. Cloudy Liquid or Sediment in Jars:

Cause: Minerals in water, overcooking, or inadequate juice clarification.

Solution: Use distilled or softened water, follow recommended processing times, and clarify juices before using.

9. Unsealed Jars Post-Processing:

Cause: Insufficient processing time, failure to heat jars properly before filling, or defective lids.

Solution: Process jars for the recommended time, preheat jars, and ensure lids are not damaged before use.

10. Loss of Liquid in Syrups or Brines:

Cause: Overcooking or using a syrup/brine that is too weak.

Solution: Follow recommended syrup/brine recipes, avoid overcooking, and maintain correct ratios.

Color Changes in Preserves

Color changes in preserves, such as jams, jellies, and fruit-based products, can occur due to various factors. While these changes are generally harmless, understanding the causes can help you maintain the desired appearance of your canned goods.

1. Oxidation:

Cause: Exposure to air during processing or storage.

Solution: Ensure jars are filled quickly, remove air bubbles, and apply lids promptly. Store jars in a cool, dark place to minimize oxidation.

2. Fruit Ripeness:

Cause: Using overly ripe or under-ripe fruit.

Solution: Choose fruit at its peak ripeness. Under-ripe fruit may lead to a dull color, while overly ripe fruit can cause browning.

3. Natural Changes Over Time:

Cause: Fruits may naturally change color over time due to exposure to light and air.

Solution: Store preserves in a cool, dark place and consume within the recommended time frame.

4. Pectin Reaction:

Cause: Pectin sensitivity to pH and sugar content.

Solution: Follow recipes precisely, as changes in acidity or sugar levels can affect the color. Use commercial pectin as directed.

5. Cooking Duration:

Cause: Overcooking can lead to a darker color.

Solution: Follow recommended cooking times. Overcooking can cause caramelization and alter the color and flavor.

6. Fruit Variety:

Cause: Different varieties of fruits can produce varying colors.

Solution: Embrace the natural color variations of different fruit varieties. Mixing fruits may result in unique hues.

7. Use of Artificial Additives:

Cause: Artificial colorings can affect the final color.

Solution: If using artificial additives, follow recommended quantities. Consider natural alternatives for coloring, such as beet juice or saffron.

8. Mineral Content in Water:

Cause: Water with high mineral content may impact color.

Solution: Use distilled or soft water, especially when preparing syrups, brines, or cooking fruits.

9. Fruit Skins and Peels:

Cause: Leaving skins or peels on can influence color.

Solution: Peel fruits if a consistent color is desired. Some recipes may benefit from leaving peels for added flavor and color complexity.

10. Temperature During Processing:

Cause: Drastic temperature changes during processing can affect color.

Solution: Allow jars to cool gradually to prevent shock-induced changes.

11. Browning:

Cause: Enzymatic browning in fruits.

Solution: Some browning is natural and harmless. Adding lemon juice or ascorbic acid can help prevent browning.

12. Fruit Maturity at Harvest:

Cause: Harvesting fruits before they are fully mature.

Solution: Allow fruits to ripen fully on the plant before harvesting.

Tips for Preserving Color:

1) Process fruits and preserves swiftly to minimize exposure to air.

2) Select fresh, ripe fruits at their peak.

3) Adhere to recommended ingredients and ratios in recipes.

4) Keep preserves in a cool, dark place to maintain color.

5) If needed, use natural coloring agents like beet juice or carrot juice.

6) Understanding the factors that influence color changes in preserves allows you to make informed decisions during the canning process. While color changes are natural, following best practices and optimizing fruit selection can help you achieve vibrant and appealing preserves.

Preventing Spoilage in Canned Goods:

Ensuring the safety and quality of home-canned goods is essential to prevent spoilage and potential health risks. Here are key practices to follow for preventing spoilage:

1. Use Approved Recipes:

Utilize recipes from reputable sources, such as canning guides, extension services, or trusted cookbooks. Approved recipes ensure proper pH levels, acidity, and processing times for safe canning.

2. Sterilize Equipment:

Sterilize jars, lids, and utensils before use. This reduces the risk of introducing harmful bacteria or contaminants into the preserved food.

3. Inspect Jars for Damage:

Check jars for cracks, chips, or defects that may compromise the seal. Damaged jars may lead to spoilage.

4. Maintain Proper Headspace:

Follow recommended headspace guidelines in recipes. Incorrect headspace can impact sealing and increase the risk of spoilage.

5. Use Fresh, High-Quality Ingredients:

Choose fresh, high-quality produce for canning. Overripe or damaged fruits and vegetables may already contain spoilage microorganisms.

6. Follow Processing Times and Methods:

Adhere to recommended processing times and methods specified in the recipe. Under-processing can lead to inadequate heat penetration, increasing the risk of spoilage.

7. Check Altitude Adjustments:

Adjust processing times for altitude, as recommended for your specific location. High altitudes may require longer processing times.

8. Monitor Temperature:

Maintain a consistent temperature during processing. Rapid temperature changes can impact the sealing and contribute to spoilage.

9. Avoid Overfilling Jars:

Leave the specified headspace in jars to allow for proper expansion during processing. Overfilled jars may not seal correctly.

10. Cool Jars Gradually:

Allow jars to cool naturally after processing. Rapid cooling can cause siphoning and compromise seals.

11. Store in a Cool, Dark Place:

Store canned goods in a cool, dark, and dry place. Exposure to light and heat can degrade the quality of the food.

12. Regularly Check Seals:

Inspect jar seals regularly. If the seal is broken or compromised, the contents may be spoiled. Discard any jars with compromised seals.

13. Rotate and Consume Within Recommended Time:

Practice FIFO (first in, first out) by rotating your canned goods. Consume items within the recommended time frame to ensure optimal quality.

14. Be Aware of Signs of Spoilage:

Look for signs of spoilage, such as off odors, mold growth, or unusual discoloration. If in doubt, discard the contents.

15. Educate Yourself:

Stay informed about safe canning practices. Attend canning workshops, read updated guidelines, and consult with extension services or experienced canners.

16. Use Proper Water:

When preparing brines, syrups, or cooking fruits, use distilled or soft water to prevent mineral content from impacting the final product.

17. Acidify Low-Acid Foods:

For low-acid foods, such as vegetables and meats, ensure proper acidification. Add lemon juice or vinegar according to recommended guidelines.

18. Regularly Update Canning Knowledge:

Stay updated on canning recommendations and guidelines. New research may provide insights into improved safety practices.

19. Avoid Unapproved Shortcuts:

Avoid shortcuts not recommended in approved recipes, such as reducing processing times or altering ingredient proportions.

20. Consult Experts:

Seek advice from experienced canners, extension services, or food safety authorities for specific questions or concerns. By following these preventive measures, you can significantly reduce the risk of spoilage in your home-canned goods and ensure the safety and quality of the preserved food.

Made in United States
Troutdale, OR
04/30/2024

19543161R10035